Other titles by Stephen Gaukroger:

It Makes Sense
A popular, humourous and compelling look at the reasons why it does make sense to be a Christian. (Scripture Union)

Why Bother with Mission? (IUP)

Battleground (Christian Focus Publications)

Acts (Crossway)

Double Cream

STEPHEN GAUKROGER AND NICK MERCER

MONARCH
BOOKS

Originally published as *Frogs in Cream* and *Frogs II*
by Scripture Union, 130 City Road, London, EC1V 2NJ

This combined edition with new material published 1998

British Library Cataloguing Data
A catalogue record for this book is available
from the British Library.

ISBN 1 85424 399 3

Designed and produced by Bookprint Creative Services
P.O. Box 827, BN21 3YJ, England for
MONARCH BOOKS
in association with
ANGUS HUDSON LTD
Concorde House, Grenville Place, Mill Hill
London, NW7 3SA.
Printed in Great Britain.

Acknowledgements

We gratefully acknowledge the many
speakers – good, bad and indifferent – which
it has been our pleasure to listen to over the
years. Especially those who know
how to tell a story.

Contents

The Art of Illustration

'I sometimes think he tries a bit too hard
at family services!'

1

Illustrations: finding and using them

To most modern congregations, illustrations are like the ketchup on the burger, the cream on the strawberries or the chocolate flake in the ice-cream. You can exist without them but it's so much 'tastier' when they are there! Most speakers know the value of good illustrations — but where do you get them from? Well, you could:

- Develop your powers of observation. Daily life is a rich source of funny, sad and poignant incidents. Train yourself to look for them.
- Keep pen and paper handy. Write down possible illustrations as you come across them on TV, in the paper, in the shower or in general reading.
- Read biographies. People are interested in other people . . . particularly famous other people!
- 'Steal' them from other speakers!
- Use the little stories at the bottom of the page in the *Readers' Digest*.
- Subscribe to *Church News Service*, a magazine

which will keep you supplied with features, quotes, ideas and illustrations. (*Church News Service*, 37B New Cavendish Street, London W1M 8JR.)

Illustrations usually need to 'illustrate' but occasionally they can be used effectively simply to give the congregation breathing space between the meatier sections of a sermon or talk. A short, illustrative 'mental break' is likely to increase the length of time the congregation or audience can concentrate.

Don't use too many illustrations, tell inappropriate jokes or pretend something happened to *you* when you got the story from a book! Timing is essential to watch, too: beware of giving the right illustration at the wrong time in the message. As a general rule, the nearer you get to the end of the talk, the less likely is humour to be appropriate.

Take up these suggestions, avoid the pitfalls, and then your illustrations won't be like ketchup on strawberries or chocolate flakes in your burgers!

2

Humour and the Bible

The Bible is a profoundly serious collection of
writings yet it is also full of humour of every
type, although this is sometimes lost in
translation or through familiarity. A person with
a good sense of humour almost always has good
self-insight. Perhaps this is why so many of the
Bible's writers used humour to comment
incisively and memorably on issues of immense
personal and national concern.

The Bible's humour ranges through:

- the *irony* of the Tower of Babel, built to reach
'up' to heaven — and God arranges an outing
to go 'down' to see it (Genesis 11:4–5);
- the *pun* on Ehud, the left-handed Benjamite
(Benjamin = 'son of my right hand'; Joshua
3:15);
- the 'lavatorial' *sarcasm* of Elijah on Carmel,
mocking the no-show of the god Baal —
'perhaps he's on the loo?' (1 Kings 18:27);
- the *exaggeration* of Jesus — 'It's easier to get a

camel through the eye of a needle than to get a rich person into heaven . . . !' (eg Luke 18:25);

- and even the *risqué innuendo* of Paul's barbed comment about some Jewish Christians who insisted that believers must be circumcised — 'If only the knife would slip . . . !' (Galatians 5:12).

If preaching is in part, 'truth through personality', then we, like the writers of the Bible, must use every aspect of our personality, including the gift of humour, to communicate God's truth.

3

Good and bad uses of humour

The Bible's humour is generally heavy on irony and light on sarcasm. Preachers down through the ages have sometimes taken the easy way out, though, and majored on sarcasm while ducking the harder work of irony. Even Luther and Calvin stooped to this. Spurgeon, too, the nineteenth-century prince of preachers who pulled in vast crowds, peppered his sermons with every form of wit — irony, pun, hyperbole, litotes, anecdote, parody, caricature, satire . . . and even a little sarcasm.

How can we use humour for the best advantage of our message, rather than to take advantage of others or of our position with a captive audience? Here are some suggestions of things to avoid and of ways to use humour.

Humour at its worst . . .

- is attention-seeking and reflects self-centredness.

- side-tracks a good raconteur by encouraging him to make the audience laugh even more!
- distracts an audience if used unthinkingly. A witticism may pop into the speaker's head, but speaking it out may destroy the atmosphere the Spirit was building.
- can be disastrous if accidental. For instance, a Spoonerism ('Who is a gardening pod like Thee . . .') or a *double entendre* as a result of not being street-wise in the current use of language ('It was a gay evening . . .') can cause the audience to roll around in hysterics while your serious message is lost for ever.
- is pastorally insensitive. Acts which leave people devastated, such as abortion, rape and child abuse, should never be referred to humorously. A wide range of others, including death, sex, homosexuality, feminism, politics and foreigners, can only be used with the utmost care and where you really know your audience.
- goes down like a pork pie in a synagogue if humour doesn't come naturally to you. If you're not comfortable using humour, neither will your congregation or audience be!

Humour at its best . . .

Use it:

- to illustrate the point.
- to gain a *rapport* with the audience, especially if they are unknown to you and to each other.

- to release unhelpful tension among the listeners, perhaps by defusing the pressure of a difficult subject, breaking up a long sermon or simply giving you and the audience time for a few deep breaths and a re-adjustment of clothes!
- to break through the listeners' defences, making them more open to what God has to say to them.
- to bring people down to earth, reminding us of humankind's foolishness and peeling away the pomposity and humbug with which we surround ourselves. Use humour to help us see our true, petty and paradoxical selves: full of noble aspirations and sordid fantasies — just like an impressive cathedral whose spire points us to heaven but whose gargoyles laugh down at us.
- to identify with our culture. Humour is one of the most powerful vehicles of communication in late twentieth-century western culture. People expect it, and it 'gets through' to them. Watch TV, listen to the radio, read the papers, popular magazines and books, and see how the advertisers use humour to 'sell' their wares.
- as one of God's greatest medicines for tired and anxious minds. As Malcolm Muggeridge, the former editor of *Punch* and late-in-life convert comments, 'Next to mystical enlightenment [laughter] is the most precious gift and blessing that comes to us on earth.'

The A-Z of Stories, Illustrations, Anecdotes Witticisms etc...

Rosey! I've told you never phone me at work!

A

Abilities — hitherto undiscovered

A motorist who drove his Reliant Robin three-wheeler on the M20 at 105 miles per hour was fined £150 for speeding and banned from driving for twenty-one days. Magistrates at West Malling, Kent, heard that police following the driver were so amazed that they had the speedometer of their patrol car tested. The driver, a labourer, who was also ordered to pay £80 costs, said after the hearing that he bought the V-registration Reliant for £500, and 'would not change it for anything.'

Age

Growing old isn't so bad when you consider the alternative.

Maurice Chevalier

The seven ages of man: spills, drills, thrills, bills, ills, pills, wills.

Richard J Needham

An anonymous prayer

Lord, thou knowest better than I know myself that I am growing older. Keep me from getting too talkative and thinking I must say something on every subject and on every occasion.

Release me from craving to straighten out everybody's affairs. Teach me the glorious lesson that, occasionally, it is possible that I may be mistaken.

Make me thoughtful, but not moody; helpful, but not bossy; for thou knowest, Lord, that I want a few friends at the end.

Little girl to old man with grey beard: 'Were you in the ark?'
  'Goodness, no!'
  Pause.
  'Then why weren't you drowned?'

Someone is old if he or she is twenty years older than yourself.

Three signs of getting old:
1 Greying hair.
2 Memory loss.
And 3 . . . er . . . er . . .

*I'm sure he's not using that overhead
projector properly!*

Experience is a comb life gives you when all your hair is gone.

You know you're old when you have to think about whether to bend over and pick up something you've dropped.

No. You know you're old when you bend over to pick up something and then you look round to see if there's anything else to pick up while you're down there!

No. You know you're old when, by the time you've got down there, you can't remember what it was you bent over to pick up!

Agnosticism

Did you hear about the agnostic, dyslexic, insomniac who lay awake at night wondering, 'Is there a Dog?'

Atheism

To you I'm an atheist. To God I'm the loyal opposition.

Woody Allen

Attitude

A German group of psychologists, physicians and insurance companies who co-operated on a research project designed to find the secret to long life and success, made a surprising discovery. The secret? Kiss your spouse each morning when you leave for work!

The meticulous German researchers discovered that men who kiss their wives every morning have fewer car accidents on their way to work than men who omit the morning kiss. The good-morning kissers miss less work because of sickness, and earn twenty to thirty per cent more money than non-kissers. How do they explain their findings? According to West Germany's Dr Arthur Szabo, 'A husband who kisses his wife every morning begins the day with a positive attitude.'

Authority

The Captain on the bridge of a large naval ship saw a light ahead, set for collision with his vessel. He signalled to it: 'Alter your course ten degrees south.' The reply came back: 'Alter *your* course ten degrees north.'

The Captain then signalled: 'Alter your course ten degrees south. I am a Captain.' The reply came back: 'Alter your course ten degrees north. I am a Seaman third-class.'

The Captain, furious by now, signalled back: 'Alter your course ten degrees south. I am a battleship!' The reply: 'Alter your course ten degrees north. I am a lighthouse.'

Baptism

Church bulletin: On Tuesday afternoon there will be meetings in the north and south ends of the church. Children will be baptised at both ends.

There was the Baptist minister who at his first baptism became stagestruck. Standing in the pool with the candidate, he suffered a complete lapse of memory. He became so muddled that he forgot which sacrament he was administering. Eyes heavenward, he commanded: 'Drink ye all of it!'

Baptists

At a Baptist church meeting there was heated discussion about changing the church's name from Puddlington Baptist Church to Puddlington Christian Church.

Eventually, one old boy stood up and declared, 'I've been a Baptist for over fifty years and nobody's going to start calling *me* a Christian!'

How many Baptists does it take to change a light bulb?

A church meeting and about two-and-a-half years.

Billy Graham is sitting quietly in a restaurant one day when a hold-up man comes in brandishing a gun. 'Okay. I want everyone to file past me and hand me their wallets.' When Billy Graham arrives in front of the robber, the man recognises him and motions the evangelist to put his wallet back in his pocket. 'Put it away, Billy,' he says. 'We Baptists must stick together!'

Bible

The Bible is so good, if it isn't true it ought to be!

A theologically liberal minister was visiting one of the elderly members of his congregation. He noticed that her Bible had hundreds of pages torn out of it, while many others had been cut up.

'What happened to your Bible?' he asked.

'Oh,' she replied, 'I just tear out all the bits you say we can't believe any more.'

No one ever graduates from Bible study until he meets its Author face to face.

Everett Harris

The ten commandments

People nowadays treat the ten commandments like a history exam . . . they attempt only three.

Psalms and Proverbs

David and Solomon lived right merry lives.
One had a thousand concubines, the other a
   thousand wives.
But when, as they were growing old, they began
   to have their qualms,

'Is there a version in Vulcan yet?'

The one wrote the Proverbs and the other wrote the Psalms.

Beatitudes for the twentieth century
(Matthew 5)

Blessed are the pushers, for they get on in the world.
Blessed are the hard-boiled, for they never let life hurt them.
Blessed are they who complain, for they get their way in the end.
Blessed are the blasé, for they never worry over their own sins.
Blessed are the slave-drivers, for they get results.
Blessed are the trouble-makers, for they make people notice them.

J B Phillips

John's Gospel

John's Gospel is 'like a magic pool where a child can paddle and an elephant can swim.'

Francis Moloney

If you can't convince 'em with Matthew, Mark, Luke or John . . . hit 'em with the Acts!

Bible: ignorance of

An RE teacher asked a pupil, 'Who knocked down the walls of Jericho?'

'I didn't, Sir; I was away last week.'

So the teacher went to the headmaster. 'Who knocked down the walls of Jericho?' he asked.

'I'm not sure,' said the headmaster. 'I'll come back to you on that one.'

The headmaster wrote to the Minister of Education, 'Who knocked down the walls of Jericho?' he asked.

Eventually he received the reply, 'You just get the wall rebuilt and we'll see that someone pays the bill.'

Bible study

'We'll carry on discussing it over cake and coffee, then at 9.00pm we'll have some feedback. . .'

The story is told of a South Sea Islander who proudly displayed his Bible to a GI during World

War II. Rather disdainfully, the soldier commented, 'We've grown out of that sort of thing.' The Islander smiled and said, 'It's a good thing we haven't. If it weren't for this book, you'd have been a meal by now!'

Books

A man goes into the cinema and buys a ticket for himself and his dog. The usher is amazed to see the dog laughing throughout the film. After the show she comments to the man as he leaves, 'I was staggered to see your dog laughing at the film!' The man replies, 'So was I. He hated the book!'

Brevity

A large dinner party was organised to pay homage to a distinguished man. He spoke to the host beforehand and asked whether, in response to the eulogy, he wanted him to give his short speech or his long speech. The host, not surprisingly, asked for the short speech.

At the close of the dinner and after all the words of praise, the guest stood up and said, 'Thank you!'

The host approached him afterwards and

I take it, brother, you've always carried your
Bible under your **left** arm?

asked him what his long speech would have been. 'Thank you very much!' he replied.

Brevity of life

A notice from the obituary column:
   DIED: Salvador Sanchez, 23, World Boxing Council featherweight champion and one of the sport's best fighters; of injuries after his Porsche 928 collided with two trucks, just north of Queretaro, Mexico. A school dropout at 16, Sanchez once explained, 'I found out that I liked hitting people, and I didn't like school, so I started boxing.' A peppery tactician, he wore opponents down for late-round knockouts. His record: 43–1–1.
   'I'd like to step down undefeated,' he said last month. 'I'm only 23 and I have all the time in the world.'

Busyness

Busyness rapes relationships. It substitutes shallow frenzy for deep friendships. It promises satisfying dreams but delivers hollow nightmares. It feeds the ego but starves the inner man. It fills a calendar or diary but fractures a

It's my new Swiss Army crozier!

family. It cultivates a programme but plows under priorities.
(*Charles Swindoll*, Killing Giants, Pulling Thorns)

Calling

Memorandum

TO: Jesus, son of Joseph, woodcrafter, Carpenter's Shop, Nazareth.

FROM: Jordan Management Consultants, Jerusalem.

Dear Sir
Thank you for submitting the résumés of the twelve men you have picked for management positions in your new organisation. All of them have now taken our battery of tests; we have not only run the results through our computer, but also arranged personal interviews for each of them with our psychologist and vocational aptitude consultant.

It is the staff opinion that most of your nominees are lacking in background, education and vocational aptitude for the type of enterprise you are undertaking. They do not have the team concept. We would recommend that you continue your search for persons of experience in managerial ability and proven capability.

Simon Peter is emotionally unstable and given to fits of temper.

Andrew has absolutely no qualities of leadership.

The two brothers, *James and John*, the sons of Zebedee, place personal interest above company loyalty.

Thomas demonstrates a questioning attitude that would tend to undermine morale.

We feel it is our duty to tell you that *Matthew* has been blacklisted by the Greater Jerusalem Better Business Bureau.

James, son of Alphaeus, and *Thaddaeus* definitely have radical leanings, and they both registered a high score on the manic-depressive scale.

One of the candidates, however, shows great potential. He is a man of ability and resourcefulness, meets people well, has a keen business mind and has contacts in high places. He is highly motivated, ambitious and responsible. We recommend *Judas Iscariot* as your controller and right-hand man. All of the other profiles are self-explanatory.

We wish you success in your new venture.

God buries his workmen but carries on his work.
Charles Wesley

While women weep, as they do now, I'll fight; while little children go hungry, I'll fight; while men go to prison, in and out, as they do now, I'll fight; while there is a drunkard left, while there is a poor, lost girl upon the streets, where there remains one dark soul without the light of God — I'll fight! I'll fight to the very end!
William Booth

Calvary

Calvary is a telescope through which we look into the long vista of eternity and see the love of God breaking forth into time.
Martin Luther King, Jr

Change

A Ghanaian newspaper is reputed to have recorded the following piece of news: 'Ghana is to change over to driving on the right. The change will be made gradually.'

One minister to another at a fraternal: 'I can't stand change, especially in the collection!'

I have examined myself thoroughly and have come to the conclusion that I do not need to change much.

Sigmund Freud

There can be stress without change, but no change without stress.

The seven last words of the church: 'We've never done it that way before!'

If the good Lord had wanted us to go metric, he would have had only ten apostles.

Half-way through the church meeting of his tiny Irish congregation, the new minister had a quiet word with the church secretary. 'Do you have a word in Celtic for *mañana*?' he asked.

'Yes,' replied the secretary, 'but it lacks the sense of urgency.'

There are three types of people: those who make things happen; those who watch things happen, and those who haven't a clue what's happening!

Character

The way to gain a good reputation is to endeavour to be what you desire to appear.

Socrates

It is right to be contented with what we have, never with what we are.

Sir James Mackintosh

Character is what you are in the dark.

D L Moody

Charismatics

How many Charismatics does it take to change a light bulb?
  Five: one to change the bulb and four to share the experience.

Children

The learned teach the child; the wise listen to him.

There was a blinding flash of lightning and Emily, aged five, rushed into the house, shouting:
  'Mummy, Mummy, God has just taken my picture!'

Church

The frenzied activities of evangelical Christians have become legendary. Thankfully, someone has now revised the old nursery rhyme so that it fits today's picture:

Mary had a little lamb,
'Twas given her to keep,
But then it joined the Baptist Church
And died for lack of sleep.

The three vicars were discussing techniques for trying to rid their church towers of bats — messy (but protected) little creatures.

'I tried putting netting up and then taking them miles away before releasing them', said one, 'but they always find their way back'.

'Oh I always let rip with a shotgun — just warning shots — and they fly away,' said another.

'Does that really work?'

'No. Within a day or two they're settled back in the tower.'

'I have no problems,' said the third. 'I catch them one at a time, then baptise and confirm them, and I never see them again.'

Church life

Things go right gradually, they go wrong all at once.

Church growth

In the thrombosis of the church the minister is often the clot.

'Veni, vidi, velcro.' I came, I saw, I stuck around.

Those who fail to plan, plan to fail.

Could it be that just a few church members are like Pat the Irishman . . .?

Two Irishmen on a tandem eventually arrived, perspiring, at the top of a long hill.

'That was a stiff climb, Pat,' said one.

'It was that,' said Pat, 'and if I hadn't kept the brake on we would have gone backwards for sure.'

A new vicar regularly spent five days of the week in the graveyard, cutting the grass and tidying up. The church council eventually questioned him about this and he replied, 'As five-sevenths of my income come from the dead,

I thought I'd spend five-sevenths of my time with them!'

A group of clergymen were discussing whether or not they ought to invite Dwight L Moody to their city. The success of the famed evangelist was brought to the attention of the men.

One unimpressed minister commented, 'Does Mr Moody have a monopoly on the Holy Ghost?'

Another man quietly replied, 'No, but the Holy Ghost seems to have a monopoly on Mr Moody.'

Growing pains

A man got talking to a new colleague and discovered he had six children.

'I wish *I* had six kids', he said ruefully.

'How many do you have, then?' asked his colleague.

'Twelve!'

A slightly cynical minister, on his first flight in a Jumbo Jet, said that it reminded him of his church: several hundred people sitting back looking bored and a few stewards and crew members rushed off their feet!

> Some go to church to take a walk;
> Some go to church to laugh and talk;
> Some go there to meet a friend;
> Some go there their time to spend;
> Some go there to meet a lover;
> Some go there a fault to cover;
> Some go there for speculation;
> Some go there for observation;
> Some go there to doze and nod;
> The wise go there to worship God.

Church music

When a man from the country returned from a visit to the city, he told his wife, Mary, that he had gone to church and that the choir had sung an anthem.

Mary asked, 'What's an anthem?'

Her husband replied, 'Well, it's like this. If I said, 'Mary, the cows are in the corn', that would be like a hymn. But if I said, 'Oh Mary! Mary! Mary! The cows are in the corn, the Jersey cow, the Ayrshire cow, the Muley cow; all the cows, all the cows, the cows, the cows are in the corn, the corn, the corn,' then that would be an anthem!'

Anglican Digest

Class distinction

It was the sort of area where they had grapes on the sideboard when no one was ill. And even the Fire Brigade was ex-directory.

It was a rough area, but in the vanguard of the Green movement — they had had lead-free churches for 30 years.

Commitment

We know what happens to people who stay in the middle of the road: they get run over.

Aneurin Bevan

Seen on an American car bumper: 'If you love Jesus, tithe! Any fool can honk!'

Communication

The Revd W A Spooner, the English scholar who died in 1930, was reputed to have had a dreadful habit of confusing his message in the process of giving it:

On one occasion he announced to his congregation that the next hymn would be, 'From Iceland's greasy mountains.'

At a wedding he told the groom, 'It is kistomary to cuss the bride.'

Calling on the dean of Christ Church he asked the secretary, 'Is the bean dizzy?'

Giving the eulogy at a cleryman's funeral, he praised his departed colleague as a 'shoving leopard to his flock.'

In a sermon he warned his congregation, 'There is no peace in a home where a dinner swells', meaning, of course, 'where a sinner dwells.'

Speaking to a group of farmers, Spooner intended to greet them as 'sons of toil,' but what came out was, 'I see before me tons of soil.'

One of the early Anglican charismatics, Michael Harper, was introduced on American TV as 'the angelican leader of the cosmetic revival'!

*I'm so terribly sorry but we've had nothing
but problems since we installed a computer!!*

A sign in three languages in the Swiss village of Chateau d'Oex shows the impossibility of arriving at common European standards. In English, it says, 'Please do not pick the flowers.' In German: 'It is forbidden to pick the flowers.' In French: 'Those who love the mountains, leave them their flowers.'

The Times, 4 June 1992

Six-year old Margaret asked her father when their new baby would talk. He told her that it would not be for two years, since little babies don't talk.

'Oh yes they do!' Margaret insisted. 'Even in the Bible they do!'

'What makes you say that?' he asked.

'When the lady read the Bible this morning in church, she definitely said that Job cursed the day he was born!'

And God said to Noah: 'Will you build me an Ark?'

'Yes, Lord. You know that I will. But there's just one question, Lord.'

'Yes, Noah?'

'What's an Ark?'

Signing the register at a wedding, the best man had difficulty in making his ball-point pen work. 'Put your weight on it,' said the vicar. He duly signed: 'John Smith (ten stone, four pounds).'

A man went round to the tradesman's entrance of a big house and asked if they had any odd jobs that he could do. After a moment's thought the owner said he would pay him £25 to go round to the front of the house and paint the porch.

After only a couple of hours the man came back with the pot of white paint and declared that he had finished the job.

'That was very quick!' exclaimed the owner.

'Yes, well it's not all that big — and, by the way, it's a Mercedes, not a Porsche!'

A young man was about to be married, but it wasn't until the night before the wedding that he tried on his suit. The rest of the family were horrified to see that the trousers were three inches too long. But the young man declared he couldn't care less, went to bed and fell fast asleep.

At about midnight, his sister was wide awake, worrying. So she sneaked into his room, cut three inches off the trouser legs, hemmed them up neatly and went back to bed satisfied.

At three in the morning, his mother, who hadn't slept a wink, got up, slipped into her son's room, and took three inches off the trouser legs. She hemmed them up then crept quietly back to bed again.

At six in the morning, Grandma was up bright and early; took the chance while her grandson was asleep to go quietly into his room, take three inches off the wedding trouser, and . . .

Conformity

He who marries the spirit of the age is sure to be a widower in the next.

G K Chesterton

Consumerism as Religion

Sainsbury's gets more like Heaven every day; members of staff airily salute you with 'Would you like to claim your Reward?'

Eric Griffiths reviews A History of Heaven

'Tesco ergo sum.' I shop, therefore I am.

'It's very nice, but did we *really* need stone cladding? !'

Convictions

Give us clear vision that we may know where to stand and what to stand for, because unless we stand for something, we shall fall for anything.

Peter Marshall

Conversion

Conversion is an initial event which must become a continuous process, not something static and frozen, but a dynamic, ongoing process.

Bishop George Appleton

Ten reasons why I never wash

1 I was made to wash as a child.
2 People who wash are hypocrites — they reckon they're cleaner than other people.
3 There are so many different kinds of soap, I could never decide which one was right.
4 I used to wash, but it got boring, so I stopped.
5 I still wash on special occasions, like Christmas and Easter.
6 None of my friends wash.

7 I'm still young. When I'm older and have got
   a bit dirtier I might start washing.
8 I really don't have time.
9 The bathroom's never warm enough.
10 People who make soap are only after your
   money.

Daft, isn't it? We all need to wash, and we know
it. There's no argument!

And we all need a personal friendship with
Jesus, too. The need may not be quite so obvious,
but it's there all the same.

Jesus can do something soap and water can
never do: he can make us clean *on the inside*! And
that can't be bad.

Like to know how he does it? We'd be glad to
explain — without any flannel or soft soap!
Christian Publicity Organistion, Worthing

Philosophers have only interpreted the world
differently; the point is, however, to change it.
Karl Marx

A converted cannibal is one who, on Fridays,
eats only fishermen.

'To be honest, it's the finest notice board
in the country . . .'

Two caterpillars were sitting on a cabbage leaf, looking up at a beautiful butterfly, and one said to the other, 'You'll never get me up in one of those things!'

Revolution transforms everything except the human heart.

Victor Hugo

Why Communism failed: Communism decrees, 'On every man a new suit.' Christianity says, 'In every suit a new man.'

Covering your tracks

A minister wrote: 'Don't be surprised if you find mistakes in this church newsletter. We print something for everyone. And some people are always looking for mistakes.'

Creation

Teacher: 'How did the universe come into being?'

Student: 'I'm terribly sorry, sir; I'm sure I did know, but I'm afraid I've forgotten.'

Teacher: 'How very unfortunate. Only two persons have ever known how the universe came into being: the Author of Nature and yourself. Now one of the two has forgotten!'

The Cross

Our hope lies not in the man we put on the moon, but in the man we put on the cross.

Don Basham

D

Death

My grandfather would look through the obituary columns and say to me, 'Strange, isn't it, how everybody seems to die in alphabetical order?'

I'm not afraid to die; I just don't want to be there when it happens.

Woody Allen

I don't want to achieve immortality through my work; I want to achieve it by not dying.

Woody Allen

Obviously one isn't indestructible — quite.

Margaret Thatcher, 1988

Dr Donald Grey Barnhouse told of the occasion when his first wife had died. He was driving his

children home from the funeral service.
Naturally, they were overcome with grief and Dr
Barnhouse was trying hard to think of some
word of comfort to give them. Just then, a huge
truck passed them. As it did so, its shadow
swept over the car, and as it passed on in front an
idea came to him.

'Children,' he said, 'Would you rather be run
over by a truck or by its shadow?' They replied,
'The shadow, of course; that can't hurt us at all.'
So Dr Barnhouse then said, 'Did you know that
two thousand years ago the truck of death ran
over the Lord Jesus . . . in order that only its
shadow might run over us?'

Two little girls tiptoed past their grandmother.
'Why is Granny always reading the Bible?'
asked Kate.

'Ssh!' whispered Lizzie, 'we mustn't disturb
her! She's cramming for her finals.'

'Grandpa, grandpa' says the little girl, 'please
make a noise like a frog!'

'Why do you want me to do that?' says the
exasperated grandparent as the little girl persists.

'Because mummy and daddy said that when
you croaked we could all go to Disneyland in
America.'

Denominations

For Baptists, 'the priesthood of all believers'
means that even the Pope is sometimes right.

A man ran to stop another man from flinging
himself off a bridge into a river.

'Why are you killing yourself?' he asked.

'I've nothing to live for!'

'Don't you believe in God?'

'Yes, I do.'

'What a coincidence — so do I! Are you a Jew
or a Christian?

'A Christian.'

'What a coincidence — so am I! Protestant or
Catholic?'

'Protestant.'

'What a coincidence — so am I! Anglican or
Baptist?'

'Baptist.'

'What a coincidence — so am I! Strict and
Particular, or General?'

'Strict and Particular.'

'What a coincidence — so am I! Premillennial
or Amillennial?'

'Premillennial.'

'What a coincidence — so am I! Partial rapture
or Full rapture?'

'Partial rapture.'

At this, the first man sprang on the second and pushed him into the river, shouting 'Die, infidel!"

A strict Baptist visiting Newmarket finds himself at the race course and, knowing that nobody knows him there, decides to have a flutter. He goes to the paddock first and is intrigued to see a Catholic priest praying in Latin over a horse. He is even more surprised when it wins. The priest prays over two or three more horses and they all win. So finally, the Baptist lays half the church funds on the horse the priest next prays over. The horse starts well but then keels over before the first fence. The Baptist is distraught and rushes to ask the priest what happened. 'Ah, that's the trouble with you Baptists,' the priest replies, 'you don't know the difference between a blessing and the last rites!'

There was once a preacher, a Baptist and a staunch Baptist at that. No other denomination was really *Christian* in his view. If you weren't a Baptist — well, you were just the pits! He went to preach at a church that was preparing to take part in a week of prayer for Christian unity. At the end of the meeting he asked,

'How many people in this church are Baptist?'

It was a Baptist church and, knowing his

reputation, almost all the local non-Baptists had stayed away. So nearly everyone in the congregation put up their hands — all except one little old lady.

The preacher decided to embarrass her. He told the others to put their hands down and he said to her,

'What denomination are you?'

'I'm a Methodist,' she replied.

'A *what*?'

'A Methodist,' she said.

'And *why* are you a Methodist?' he asked.

'Well,' she said, 'my father was a Methodist and my grandfather was a Methodist, so I'm a Methodist.'

The preacher decided that he would really make his point here, so he said,

'That's simply ridiculous! Suppose your father was a moron and your grandfather was a moron, what would *that* make you?'

The little old lady thought for a moment, then replied,

'I guess that would make me a Baptist!'

When they rescued the Welshman after ten years alone on the desert island, they found he had built a beautiful house and two beautiful chapels.

'But why two?' they asked.

'Well, that's the chapel I go to,' he replied, 'and that's the chapel I *don't* go to!'

Puritanism: the haunting fear that someone, somewhere, may be happy.

In an advertisement by a Hong Kong dentist:
Teeth extracted by the latest Methodists.

Diplomacy

. . . the art of letting someone else have your way.

Disappointment

On his first parachute jump the soldier receives instructions from his sergeant: 'You count to ten and then pull this cord. If the parachute fails you pull the emergency parachute cord here. And then try to land near the lorry down there — they will have a nice cup of tea waiting for you.'

The parachutist counts to ten and pulls the cord. Nothing happens. He pulls the emergency cord. Nothing happens. As he hurtles towards the lorry he is heard to mutter, 'I bet there's no cup of tea, either!'

Discipleship

By blood and origin, I am all Albanian.
My citizenship is Indian.
I am a Catholic nun.
As to my calling, I belong to the whole world.
As to my heart, I belong entirely to Jesus.

Mother Teresa

Unused truth becomes as useless as an unused
muscle.

A W Tozer

Discretion

. . . is raising one's eyebrows instead of the roof.

Dogma

Every dogma has its day.

'I'd like a suit that is appropriate for a pastor with a prosperous congregation and yet shows he is sensitive to third world issues whilst retaining authority but without too much of an American TV evangelist flavour . . .'

Doublespeak

Dialogue at a dinner party full of showbiz
personalities:
  'And what are you doing at the moment?'
  'I'm writing a book.'
  'Neither am I . . .

Dreams

   Some girls long for beauty
   And others wish for fame;
   Those that burn with ambition yearn
   To carve in stone their name.

   I have but one desire,
   And there endeavour ends:
   To get my hooks on all the books
   That I have lent to friends.

E

Education/unemployment

What are the first words of a doctoral graduate in his first job?

'Anything to go with the Big Mac and fries?'

Encouragement — results of

It may be that you don't like your church's minister. Well, here is a tested prescription by which you can get rid of him (or her):

1 Look him straight in the eye when he's preaching, and maybe say 'Amen' occasionally. He'll preach himself to death in a short time.
2 Start paying him whatever he's worth. Having been on starvation wages for years, he'll promptly eat himself to death.
3 Shake hands with him and tell him he's doing a good job. He'll work himself to death.
4 Rededicate your own life to God and ask the minister to give you some church work to do. Very likely he'll keel over with heart failure.
5 If all else fails, this one is certain to succeed: get your congregation to unite in prayer for

him. He'll soon be so effective that some larger church will take him off your hands.

Enthusiasm — misguided

He was like a lighthouse in the middle of the Pennines: brilliant, but what's it there for?'

Enthusiasm — overdone

It's easier to cool down a fanatic than warm up a corpse.

Ethics

Twentieth-century ethics can be summed up as: Do unto others before they do you!

We have grasped the mystery of the atom but we have rejected the Sermon on the Mount. We have achieved brilliance without wisdom and power without conscience. Ours is a world of nuclear giants and ethical infants.

Joseph R Sizoo

In a Paris hotel elevator: Please leave your values at the front desk.

In a Japanese hotel: You are invited to take advantage of the chambermaid.

Evangelism

A newly employed American salesman stunned his bosses with his first written report, for it demonstrated quite clearly that he was nearly illiterate. He wrote, 'I seen this outfit who aint never bought ten cents worth of nothin from us and sole them some goods. i am now going to Chicawgo.' Before they could fire him, a second report arrived and it read, 'I came to Checawgo an sole them haff a millyon.' Hesitant to dismiss the man, yet afraid of what would happen if he didn't, the sales manager transferred the problem into the President's lap.

The next day the staff were amazed to see the salesman's two reports on the bulletin board, with this memo from the President. 'We ben spendin two much time tryin to spel insted of tryin to sel. I want everybody should read these letters from Gooch, who is doin a grate job, and you should go out and do like he done!'

Doug Barnett

When I enter that beautiful city,
And the saints all around me appear,
I hope that someone will tell me
It was *you* who invited me here.

An evangelist and a pastor took a holiday together to go bear hunting in Canada. One evening the pastor was sitting in their log cabin when he heard cries for help. Looking out of the window he saw the evangelist rushing towards the hut, hotly pursued by a huge gizzly bear. The pastor jumped up to open the door to let his friend in but, at the last minute, the evangelist side-stepped the door while the grizzly bear plunged on in. As the evangelist pulled the door shut from the outside, he yelled, 'You deal with that one — I'll go and get some more!'

'I'm so sorry we can't help you with the Jumble Sale leaflets — but someone's jammed the photocopier . . .'

Facts

Facts do not cease to exist because they are ignored!

Aldous Huxley

Faith

. . . is trying to believe what you know isn't true.

. . . is sitting on a branch while the Devil is sawing through it, and believing the tree will fall down!

Faith

Three men were walking on a wall,
Feeling, Faith and Fact.
When Feeling got an awful fall,
Then Faith was taken back.
So close was Faith to Feeling,
That he stumbled and fell too,

But Fact remained and pulled Faith back,
And Faith brought Feeling too.

God sent sex to drive a man to marriage,
ambition to drive a man to service, and fear to
drive a man to faith.

Luther

To our forefathers, our faith was an experience.
To our fathers, our faith was an inheritence.
To us, our faith is a convenience.
To our children, our faith is a nuisance.

Praying Samuels come from praying Hannahs
. . . and praying leaders come from praying
homes.

Edward M Bounds

Families

'We have careful thought for the stranger
And smiles for the sometime guest
But oft for our own the bitter tone
Though we love our own the best.'

Margaret E Sangster

Fanaticism

A fanatic is someone who can't change his mind and won't change the subject.

Winston Churchill

God finds it easier to cool down a fanatic than to warm up a corpse.

George Verwer

Fighting back

A church near the flight path of London Airport displays a cartoon of Concorde flying past its steeple, with the air hostess telling the pilot, 'The passengers are complaining about the noise of the singing, sir!'

Flattery

After a loquacious and flattering introduction by his host, the speaker prays, 'Lord, forgive my brother for all the wonderful but exaggerated things he said about me, and forgive me for enjoying every word.'

Fools

Make it idiot proof and someone will make a better idiot.

Forgiveness

An Episcopal Church in the United States advertised what it had to offer: 'In the church started by a man with six wives, forgiveness goes without saying.'

Every saint has a past and every sinner has a future.

Oscar Wilde

When the Devil reminds you of your past, you remind him of his future!

Always forgive your enemies — nothing annoys them so much.

Oscar Wilde

Freedom

'Because of Christ, this wheelchair has become the prison that set me free.'

Joni Eareckson Tada

There are two kinds of freedom: the false, when a man is free to do what he likes; the true, when a man is free to do what he ought.

Charles Kingsley

Fulfilment

I may, I suppose, regard myself or pass for being a relatively successful man. People occasionally stare at me in the streets — that's fame. I can fairly easily earn enough to qualify for admission to the higher slopes of the Inland Revenue — that's success. Furnished with money and a little fame even the elderly, if they care to, may partake of trendy diversion — that's pleasure. It might happen once in a while that something I said or wrote was sufficiently heeded for me to persuade myself that it represented a serious impact on our time — that's fulfilment.

Yet I say to you — and I beg you to believe me — multiply these tiny triumphs by a million, add

them all together, and they are nothing — less
than nothing, a positive impediment —
measured against one draught of that living
water Christ offers to the spiritually thirsty,
irrespective of who or what they are.

> *Malcolm Muggeridge*

Generalisations

All generalisations are false.

Genius

In the Republic of Mediocrity, genius is
dangerous.

> *Robert Ingersoll*

Genius is the ability to reduce the complicated to
the simple.

True genius resides in the capacity for evaluation of uncertain, hazardous and conflicting information.

Winston Churchill

Paderewski, the Polish pianist, was once approached by a woman after one of his concerts. 'Paderewski,' she said, 'you are a genius!'

'Yes, madam,' he replied, 'but for many years before that, I was a drudge.'

Gifting

A dog goes into the local Job Centre. The interviewer is a little non-plussed but eventually sends him along to a circus that is in town.

Next day the dog is back again and the Job Centre man asks how he got on at the circus. 'Oh, that was no good,' replies the dog. 'They wanted a performing dog and I'm a bricklayer.'

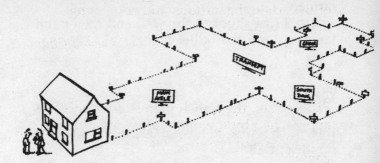

'It's a modest House Church at present — but we've got great plans!'

Giving

> Do your givin'
> While you're livin'
> Then you're knowin'
> Where it's goin'!

Goals & Aims

A farmer is showing a visitor round the farm and as they walk down the side of the barn he notices several 'targets' painted on the wall. As he looks at them he sees that each has a bullet hole right in the bullseye.

'You must have wonderful aim,' he says to the farmer.

'No. I just shoot at the wall and then paint targets round the bullet holes.'

God

It is much worse to have a false idea of God than no idea at all.

Archbishop William Temple

A German General asked an English officer why the British always won wars between them, though there was little difference in their forces.

'Because we pray to God before each battle,' said the Englishman.

'But we do, too,' the General replied.

'Surely,' replied the Englishman, 'you don't expect God to understand German, do you?'

The Grand Highway?

Sound theology

Beware: lively worship

 Avoid PCCs

 Beware: long sermons

 Prone to heresy

 Roof repairs in progress

 Average age of congregation

Adult baptism practiced

 Organ requires tuning

 Disagreement among members

Real camel in nativity plays

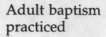 Whole families baptised

St John's Bitton, North Yorkshire

Grace

A preacher's small son had to apologize for forgetting his aunt's birthday. He wrote,

'I'm sorry I forgot your birthday. I have no excuse, and it would serve me right if you forgot mine, which is next Friday.'

Gratitude?

A farmer was showing a man round his farm one day when they came to the pig sty — and there was a magnificent pig with a wooden leg. Not surprisingly, the visitor asked about the wooden leg.

The farmer replied, 'Arr . . . now that's a very special pig. One night when we were all in bed, the farm caught fire. But that pig saw it, broke out of the sty, called the fire brigade, threw buckets of water on the fire, then rushed into the farmhouse and rescued me, my wife and the children. Yes, that's a very special pig!'

'And did he lose his leg trying to fight the fire?' enquired the visitor.

'Oh, no! But a very special pig like that — you don't eat it all at once!'

Guidance

Woman to man digging a hole in the road: 'How do you get to the Royal Albert Hall?'
'Lady, you have to practise!'

Policeman to driver going the wrong way up a one-way street: 'Didn't you see the arrows?'
Driver: 'I didn't even see the Indians!'

Guilt

Man is the only animal who blushes — or needs to!

Mark Twain

I'm afraid he's going to want to see more than just your baptism certificate and a video of your wedding!

H

Healing

An advertisement in the *Southport Visitor* read:
'A healing session by John Cain (of Birkenhead): Owing to illness: meeting cancelled.'

Peterborough, Daily Telegraph

Heaven

In our present condition the joys of heaven would be an acquired taste.

C S Lewis

A couple about to get married are killed in a car crash and end up at the Pearly Gates the day before their wedding would have taken place. They mention to St Peter that they would like a minister to marry them as soon as it was convenient. He says this will be no problem, but one hundred years later, when nothing has happened, they dare to ask him again if he could arrange the ceremony. 'I'm so sorry,' he replies, 'we're still waiting for a minister!'

Heaven is not just 'pie in the sky by and by'; it's 'steak on the plate while you wait'!

Hell

Hell is oneself;
Hell is alone, the other figures in it
merely projections. There is nothing to escape
    from
And nothing to escape to. One is always alone.
                        T S Eliot, 'The Cocktail Party'

Hindrances

A hindrance is someone who gets things off to a flying stop.

Honesty

The children in a prominent family decided to give their father a book of the family's history for a birthday present. They commissioned a professional biographer to do the work, carefully warning him of the family's 'black sheep' problem: Uncle George had been executed in the electric chair for murder. 'I can handle that situation so that there will be no embarrassment,' the biographer assured the children. 'I'll merely say that Uncle George occupied a chair of applied electronics at an important Government Institution. He was attached to his position by the strongest of ties and his death came as a real shock.'

The Hollywood film director, Sam Goldwyn, said:
   'I don't want any "yes-men" around me. I want men and women who tell me the truth, even if it costs them their jobs!'

It's such an honest town, Securicor uses mopeds.

Hope

On the English translation of a menu in a Swiss restaurant: Our wines leave you nothing to hope for.

'Why art thou so heavy, o my soul . . .'

Hope (false)

Probably nothing in the world arouses more false hope than the first four hours of a diet.

Human beings

Such is the human race. Often it does seem such a pity that Noah . . . didn't miss the boat.

Mark Twain

Humility

The *Church Times* recalls a story about the late Dr Newport White when he was Regius Professor of Divinity at Dublin. On one great occasion somebody noticed him sitting unrobed in a pew and whispered, 'Shouldn't you be in the procession?' To which the worthy Doctor replied, 'Just a little ostentatious humility.'

During the prayers in the vestry before the service, the deacon prayed: 'Lord, take our preacher this evening and just blot him out.'

A Keswick speaker started his address with the comment, 'You know, you only get to speak at Keswick twice: once on your way up, and once on your way down. It's nice to be back again!'

Corrie Ten Boom was once asked if it was difficult for her to remain humble. Her reply was this:

'When Jesus rode into Jerusalem on Palm Sunday on the back of a donkey, and everyone was waving palm branches and throwing garments on the road and singing praises, do you think that for one moment it ever entered the head of that donkey that any of that was for him?'

She continued, 'If I can be the donkey on which Jesus Christ rides in his glory, I give him all the praise and all the honour.'

Humour

Will Rogers, the American humorist, has commented that, 'Everything is funny as long as it is happening to somebody else.'

O Lord, make my enemies ridiculous!

Voltaire

Wit is a sword; it is meant to make people feel the point as well as see it.

G K Chesterton

He was a good man in the worst sense of the term.

Mark Twain

Hypocrisy

There are only two things I can't stand about him: his face.

The number one cause of atheism is Christians. Those who proclaim God with their mouths and deny him with their lifestyles is what an unbelieving world finds simply unbelievable.

Karl Rahner

A vicar was asked to take the funeral for a non church-going parishioner. 'We want a nice Christian funeral,' the family said, 'but nothing religious.'

'Touch my board once again and
I'll smash your face in!'

I

Idealism

An idealist is a man with both feet planted firmly in the air.

Franklin D Roosevelt

Identity

A group of British soldiers got lost in the desert during the Gulf Crisis. They eventually stumbled across an American Five-Star General who was surveying the field. 'Do you know where we are?' the men blurted out.

The General, very annoyed that they were improperly dressed, didn't salute or address him as 'Sir' responded with an indignant question, 'Do you know who I am?'

'Now we've got a real problem,' said one of the soldiers. 'We don't know where we are, and he doesn't know who he is!'

We have become a grandmother.

Margaret Thatcher, 4 March 1989

Immaturity

Out of the mouths of babes comes a lot of what
they should have swallowed.

Franklin B Jones

Incarnation

He became what we are that he might make us
what he is.

Athanasius,
fourth-century theologian and apologist

Inconsistency/ups and downs

A parachutist hurtles towards the ground, his
parachute having failed to open. As he fumbles
and panics he is amazed to pass a man going up.

'Do you know anything about parachutes?' he
shouts to him.

'No! Do you know anything about gas ovens?'

Indifference

They came first for the Communists, and I didn't
speak up because I wasn't a Communist. Then

they came for the Jews, and I didn't speak up because I wasn't a Jew. Then they came for the Trade Unionists, and I didn't speak up because I wasn't a Trade Unionist. Then they came for the Catholics, and I didn't speak up because I was a Protestant. Then they came for me — and there was no one left to speak up for me.

Martin Niemoller,
German pastor, victim of Nazi Concentration camp

Individualism

You are unique — just like everyone else.

In a Hong Kong supermarket: For your convenience, we recommend courteous, efficient self-service.

The Inner city

A little boy was saying his prayers on the last night before his family moved from Devon: 'Well, it's "goodbye" from me, now, God — we're going to live in London.'

Insincerity

He had a permanent SWEG — a Slimy Wet Evangelical Grin.

He was an Evangellyfish — he stung you with a gospel text and moved off smartly.

Integrity

What is morally wrong can never be politically right.

Abraham Lincoln

Intelligence

He was so clever that he didn't take a book to bed with him, he just browsed through his mind for half an hour.

Douglas Adams

'This is so exciting – I've never done a baptism for
the Mafia before!'

Interlude

. . . to wake up the congregation.

I've had a wonderful evening — but this wasn't it.

Groucho Marx

Involvement

Henry Dunant was born to wealthy parents in Switzerland in 1828. Deeply compassionate, he devoted considerable time to assisting and encouraging young people, especially the poor. When only about eighteen, he founded a Young Men's Christian Union.

Later, this sensitive person journeyed to Italy for an audience with Emperor Napoleon III, who was busy driving the Austrians out of Northern Italy. Arriving shortly after a horrendous battle, Henry Dunant couldn't believe what he saw. Some 40,000 men, wounded, dying and dead, lay scattered over a bloody terrain, for vermin and vultures to consume.

Forgetting his personal agenda, Dunant pitched in, doing whatever he could to help the overworked doctors. He subsequently wrote and spoke on the horrors of war. At last the Geneva Convention of 1864 convened to consider common problems. Twenty-two nations took part and signed accords acknowledging the neutrality of medical personnel in time of hostility. They chose as their banner and symbol a red cross on a white field. And so the Red Cross was born.

Joy

I have tried in my time to be a philosopher; but, I don't know how, cheerfulness was always breaking in.

Samuel Johnson

Justice

'I'm not interested in the bloody system! Why has he no food? Why is he starving to death?'

Bob Geldof
interviewed about starvation in Africa, 1985

Learning that her husband had betrayed her, Vera Czermak jumped out of her third-story window in Prague. The Czech newspaper, *Vicerni Prahi*, reported that Mrs Czermak was recovering in hospital, after landing on her husband, who was killed.

As a boy, Woodrow Wilson worshipped his father, who was a church minister, and was overjoyed when the stern man would allow him to come along on visits through the parish.

Later, when he was President of the United States, Wilson laughingly recalled the time when his father had taken him to see a neighbour. Seeing the horse and buggy that had brought the minister and his son, the concerned neighbour wondered aloud,

'Reverend, how is it that you're so thin and gaunt, while your horse is so fat and sleek?'

The Reverend began a modest reply but before he could say two words, his outspoken son announced, to the parishioner's dismay,

'Probably because my father feeds the horse, and the congregation feeds my father.'

'You'll soon get used to this new system:
just pick up the bar code reader at the end
of your pew and . . .'

K

Knowledge

Nothing worth knowing can be understood by
the mind.

Woody Allen

Leadership

Lead, follow, or get out of the way!

Ted Turner,
American media mogul and owner of CNN

Leisure

Personally, I have always looked on cricket as
organised loafing.

Archbishop William Temple

Lies

No man has a memory long enough to be a successful liar.

Abraham Lincoln

Life and the Spirit

The neatest, tidiest and most orderly place in town is usually the cemetery!

Uncouth life is better than aesthetic death.

Someone once asked Dwight Moody, the nineteenth-century American evangelist, 'Have you been filled with the Holy Spirit?'
   'Yes,' he replied, 'but I leak!'

Life — living a worthwhile one

If you would not be forgotten
As soon as you're dead and rotten,
Either write things worth reading
Or do things worth the writing.

Benjamin Franklin

Life with Christ is an endless hope; without him, a hopeless end.

May you live all the days of your life.

Jonathan Swift

Listening

His thoughts were slow,
His words were few and never formed to glisten.
But he was a joy to all his friends,
You should have heard him listen!

Lottery

– a tax on people who are poor at mathematics.

Love

The biggest disease today is not leprosy or tuberculosis, but rather the feeling of being unwanted, uncared for and deserted by everybody. The greatest evil is the lack of love and charity.

Mother Teresa

God doesn't love you any more after you become
a Christian . . .

> To live above with saints we love,
> Oh! That will be glory!
> To live below with saints we know,
> Well, that's a different story!

The Bible tells us to love our neighbours and also
to love our enemies, probably because they are
generally the same people.

G K Chesterton

M

Marriage

> To keep your marriage brimming
> With love in the loving cup,
> If ever you're wrong, admit it,
> If ever you're right, shut up.

Ogden Nash

*Rosey! I've told you **never** phone me at work!*

Where the warfare is the hottest
In the battlefields of life,
You'll find the Christian soldier
Represented by his wife.

A silly and childish game is one at which your
wife can beat you.

My wife and I were very happy for thirty years
— and then we met!

When the 'cooing' stops and the 'billing' begins.

The greatest thing a man can do for his children
is to love their mother.

Michael Cassidy

Marriage: it starts when you sink into his arms
and ends with your arms in his sink.

The average wife would rather have beauty than brains, because she knows that the average husband can see better than he can think.

I love the human race. All of my family belong to it, and some of my husband's family, too.

Marriage is a woman's way of calling a meeting to order.

Materialism

Let's stop loving things and using people, and start using things and loving people.

Media

Released in the United States in 1979 by Warner Brothers, the film *Jesus* has been dubbed into more than 130 languages and viewed in 155 countries by more than 355 million people. More than 200 mission agencies and denominations have used the film. By 1993 Campus Crusade, the catalyst for the translation effort, hopes to translate the film into all of the 271 languages spoken by more than one million people. Other organizations are interested in translating it into still more languages. Campus Crusade estimates that more than 30 million people have indicated decisions to follow Christ as a result of watching the film.

Television is . . . a medium. So called because it is neither rare nor well done!

Ernie Kovacs

I find television very educating. Every time somebody turns on the set I go into the other room and read a book.

Groucho Marx

Meekness

Seen on a church noticeboard: 'The meek will inherit the earth — if that's all right with you.'

Ministers

The old deacon came up to welcome the new minister after his induction.

'Yes there are quite a few House Churches on
this estate . . .'

'You know pastor,' he said, 'we'll never have a minister as good as you.'

'That's very kind of you,' the minister beamed.

'Yep. We've had five ministers here and each one's been worse than the one before. So we'll never have a minister as good as you.'

The churchwarden was waiting for the visiting preacher to arrive at the station and approached a serious looking man in a dark suit. 'Are you the visiting minister?' he asked.

'No. It's my ulcer that makes me look like this,' came the reply.

The guide was explaining to the Holy Land pilgrims how an eastern shepherd always leads his flock from the front, not from the back like western shepherds. Just then they drove past a dozen sheep being herded from behind by a man with a large staff and loud voice. The guide immediately jumped out of the coach to investigate. He soon returned, obviously relieved: 'He's a butcher, not a shepherd!'

Ministry — staying too long

A joke making the rounds in Baghdad:
Saddam is going for a drive in his limo and

seeing a long line of people outside the passport office, he tells his chauffeur, 'Stop the car, I want to talk to these people.'

But by the time he alights from his limo, most of the passport seekers have vanished.

'What happened? Where are they?' Saddam demands.

A bodyguard explained: 'Mr President, they thought you were applying for a passport to leave the country, and decided to stay.'

Ministry — shared

A curate had suffered a very difficult working relationship with his vicar over the three years of his first curacy. At last, it was time for him to leave. No more would he have to endure the stubbornness and pedantry of this impossible man. He preached his final sermon to the congregation on the text, 'Abide ye here with the ass, and I will go yonder.'

It's hard to soar with the eagles when you work with turkeys!

Ministry

Yours must be a soul-destroying job, vicar.

'Vicar,' beamed the old lady appreciatively, 'we didn't know what sin was until you came to this parish.'

Miracles

The following story, recorded by Perrott Philips, appeared in *Time Off* magazine.

Flying his private plane over Los Angeles, an eighty-year old pilot had a sudden heart attack and died at the controls. Without a moment's hesitation, the passenger, sixty-nine year old Charles Law — who had never flown a plane before — took over the wheel of the Cessna 150 and landed it safely at Upland California. 'I don't know how he did it,' said police sergeant John Cameron, who led a convoy of ambulances and fire engines to the air strip. 'It was a miracle.'

It certainly was. After he had landed, Charles Law had to be led gently from the plane. He is blind.

Misunderstanding

A man found a penguin wandering down the street, so took hold of its flipper and found the nearest policeman. 'What shall I do with it?' he asked. The policeman thought for a moment and then suggested, 'Take it round the corner to the zoo.'

The next day the policeman bumped into the man again, who was still clutching the penguin by the flipper. Before the policeman could say anything, the man smiled and said, 'Thanks for the idea about going to the zoo yesterday. I'm taking it to the pictures today!'

A chaplain was asked to visit an oriental patient in intensive care. He soon discovered that the man didn't speak English but, as he stood and held his hand, the man constantly repeated a strange-sounding phrase. The man became more and more anguished until finally he passed away, still muttering those words.

The chaplain rang up a friend who came from the east, and asked him what the phrase meant. 'Was it some last act of repentance?' he suggested.

'No,' says the friend, 'it simply means, "You're standing on my oxygen supply."'

A Welsh preacher worked himself into a frenzy preaching on Psalm 42, 'As the hart pants for the waterbrook so longs my soul after Thee.'

As he continued, he cried, 'Yes, brothers and sisters! It's your pants he wants!'

A little girl had a teddybear with a lazy eye. She called it 'Gladly', because she had sung about it in church: 'Gladly, my cross-eyed bear . . .'

Modesty

Church member to vicar after the service: 'You were really good this morning!'

Modestly, the vicar replies, 'Oh it wasn't me; it was the Lord.'

Church member: 'You weren't that good!'

Money

From a church bulletin: 'A number of buttons have been found among the coins in recent collections. In future, please rend your hearts and not your garments.

As the parishioners were leaving church after a service, one woman said, in a loud voice, 'I've nothing but praise for the new vicar!' A rather glum old sidesman who was passing overheard her and remarked, 'So I noticed when I passed you the collection bag.'

The average English cat costs £145 per year to feed — which is more than the average income of the one billion people who live in the world's fifteen poorest nations.

The trouble is that there's always too much month left at the end of the money.

No one would have remembered the Good Samaritan if he'd only had good intentions. He had money as well.

Margaret Thatcher, speech, 1980

No man is rich enough to buy back his past.

'Say — could be our lucky day! The Rose window
at York Minster has just fallen out!'

Sometimes, when you've read through a long, spiritual prayer letter, you eventually realise that it was a veiled plea for more money. Those sorts of letters demonstrate that 'faith without hints is dead.'

Money — the love of

The mourners at the funeral were left wondering whether one line of 'Guide me oh thou great Jehovah' had been deliberately mispelled — 'land my safe on Canaan's side.'

N

New Age

I was caught cheating in a metaphysics exam. I was looking into the soul of the boy next to me.
Woody Allen

My karma just ran over my dogma . . .

Time is an illusion; lunch-time doubly so.

Nostalgia and postmodernity

The future isn't what it used to be.

O

Obedience

It's hard to get your heart and your head to agree
in life. In my case, they're not even friendly.
Woody Allen

A group of American tourists were on a
conducted tour of the House of Commons when
a Labour Lord entered the central lobby, wearing
his ceremonial garb. He wanted to catch the
attention of Neil Kinnock, who was over on the
far side of the House, so he shouted, 'Neil!' And
fifty Americans dutifully knelt.

Optimism

A couple have twin sons, one of whom is a pessimist and the other an optimist. The parents decide to try to even things out for their birthday, so they give the pessimist a marvellous hi-fi system. When he unwraps it, he complains, 'With the price of CDs I'll never be able to afford any! And you'll soon be moaning about the noise . . .'

The optimist receives just a bag of horse manure. As he unwraps it, he leaps in the air with joy, crying, 'There's a pony on its way!'

> 'Twixt optimist and pessimist
> The difference is droll:
> The optimist sees the doughnut,
> The pessimist sees the hole.

An optimist? The woman who slips her feet back into her shoes when the preacher says, 'And finally . . .'

Just because you occasionally feel fed up, don't despair! Remember that the sun has a 'sinking spell' every night but rises again in the morning.

Originality

There is no such thing as an original joke.
Stephen Gaukroger and Nick Mercer

I fear I have nothing original in me — excepting original sin.

Thomas Campbell

Originality is the art of concealing your source.
Franklin Jones

P

The Pastor

Pastor, Priest, Vicar, Minister and friend . . .

Whatever we call him or her, it's still a tough job:

If he visits his flock, he's nosey.
If he doesn't he's a snob.
If he preaches longer than ten minutes, it's too
  long.
If he preaches less than ten minutes, he can't
  have prepared his sermon.
If he runs a car , he's worldly.
If he doesn't, he's always late for appointments.
If he tells a joke, he's flippant.
If he doesn't, he's far too serious.
If he starts the service on time, his watch must be
  fast.
If he's a minute late, he's keeping the congrega-
  tion waiting.
If he takes a holiday, he's never in the parish.
If he doesn't, he's a stick-in-the-mud.
If he runs a gala or bazaar, he's money mad.
If he doesn't, there's no social life in the parish.
If he has the Church painted and redecorated,
  he's extravagant.
If he doesn't, the Church is shabby.
If he's young, he's inexperienced.

If he's getting old, he ought to retire.
But . . .

When he dies, there's never been anyone like
him!

Adapted from Beda Review, via *Catholic Herald*

According to a writer in *Parson and Parish*, when
churches seek a new incumbent they expect, 'the
strength of an eagle, the grace of a swan, the
gentleness of a dove, the friendliness of a
sparrow and the night hours of an owl . . . Then
when they catch the bird, they expect him to live
on the food of a canary.'

How many pastors does it take to change a light
bulb?

Only one — but the bulb has really got to want
to change.

Two Yorkshire farmers were discussing their
respective clerics. One said: 'Our fellow's got
foot and mouth disease. 'E don't visit and 'e can't
preach!'

. . . It's going to be one of those days . . .

A minister's job is to comfort the afflicted and to afflict the comfortable!

The Deacon's prayer: 'Lord, send us a poor, humble minister. You keep him humble and we'll keep him poor.'

A new shorthand code for churches trying to decide what sort of minister they are looking for:

A YUMMY: A young upwardly mobile minister.

A MUMMY: A middle-aged upwardly mobile minister.

A GUMMY: A geriatric upwardly mobile minister.

The evangelist's job is to get people out of Egypt. The pastor's job is to get Egypt out of the person.

The task of pastoral ministry is, above all else, to arrange the contingencies for an encounter with the Divine.

Dietrich Bonhoeffer

Permissiveness

We cannot have permissiveness in sex and expect that we will not have permissiveness in violence, or in tax avoidance, or corruption and bribery in high places. People today want permissiveness in the bedroom but not in the board rooms; in the casino, but not in the bank. If we promote

permissiveness where we want it, we find
permissiveness where we do not want it.

Sir Frederick Catherwood

Persistence

I am extraordinarily patient, provided I get my
own way in the end.

Margaret Thatcher,
quoted in 'The Observer', January 1983

Frogs in cream

Two frogs fell into a can of cream,
Or so I've heard it told;
The sides of the can were shiny and steep,
The cream was deep and cold.

'Oh, what's the use?' croaked Number 1,
'Tis fate; no help's around.
Goodbye, my friends! Goodbye, sad world!'
And, weeping still, he drowned.

But Number 2, of sterner stuff,
Dog-paddled in surprise,
The while he wiped his creamy face
And dried his creamy eyes.

'I'll swim awhile, at least,' he said,
Or so I've heard he said;

'It really wouldn't help the world
If one more frog were dead.'

An hour or two he kicked and swam,
Not once he stopped to mutter;
But kicked and kicked and swam and kicked,
Then hopped out, via butter!

T C Hamlet

If you're ever tempted to give up, just think of
Brahms. He took seven years to compose his
famous lullaby — he kept falling asleep at the
piano!

Robert Orben

By perseverence the snail reached the Ark.

Spurgeon

Consider the postage stamp: its usefulness
consists in the ability to stick to one thing until it
gets there.

Josh Billings

Seen on the side of an ice-cream van: 'Often
licked but never beaten!'

I was leading 'choruses with actions',
if you must know!

Personality

A well-balanced person? Someone who has a chip on both shoulders.

As the little girl prayed: 'Dear God, please make all the bad people good, and please make all the good people nice.'

The Personal touch

Here is a love story. A young man and a young woman were deeply in love and, while he was away with the Navy for three years, he wrote to her every day, without fail. At the end of the three years came the happy wedding — she married the postman.

Pessimism

A pessimist is the person who looks through the obituary column in the newspaper to see if his name is there yet.

'I'm sorry, I've nothing left for the 6.30pm
Prayer and Praise, but I can let you have
two seats behind a pillar for the
11.00am Family Worship.'

We are born naked, wet and hungry. Things go
downhill from then on.

Pets

Dogs come when called.
Cats take a message and get back to you later.

Cats know how we feel.
They don't give a damn, but they know.

Pluralism

I think I need to pray; know any good religions?
Douglas Adams

All roads may lead to Rome but only one ends
up in heaven.

Mark Green

Politically correct speak

Cerebrally non-motivated (stupid)
Chronologically gifted (old)

Differently sized (fat)
Follicularly challenged (bald)
Knowledgably dispossessed (mistaken)
Hesychastic truths perceived through ontological
 media (certainty)
Atonally exciting (off key)

Politics

Capitalism is man's exploitation of man, whereas
communism is the exact opposite.

Potential

One can count the number of seeds in an apple,
but one cannot count the number of apples in a
seed.

Llandridod Wells Church magazine

Poverty

When you're down and out, something always
turns up — and it's usually the noses of your
friends.

Orson Welles

Power

Of all forces, violence is the weakest.

Gobineau

Praise

Praise undeserved is satire in disguise.

Prayer

A mother overheard her young son praying one day: '. . . and if you give me a bike, Lord, then I'll be good for a whole week.'

She interrupted him and said, 'Now, Johnny, it's no good trying to bargain with God. He won't answer prayers like that!'

A few days later she overheard him praying again: '. . . and if you give me a new bike, Lord, I'll be good for *three* weeks!'

'Johnny,' said his mother gently, 'I thought I told you it was no good trying to strike bargains with the Lord. He doesn't respond to that sort of prayer.'

A few days later the mother was cleaning the house and, to her amazement, found right at the bottom of the airing cupboard, a little statue of the madonna that had stood on the sideboard. She guessed that this must be something to do with Johnny and went up to his room to find him. He wasn't there but on the window sill she found a note which read; 'OK, Lord, if you ever want to see your mother again . . .!'

I can concentrate better when my knees are bent.

Heard at the prayer meeting: 'Lord, it was such a fantastic meeting last Saturday! All the things that happened and the "words" we got . . . You should've been there, Lord!'

The nineteenth-century Baptist preacher, Charles Spurgeon, was once asked, 'When should I pray? Should I pray when I don't feel like it?'

He replied, 'Pray when you feel like it, because God will bless you; pray when you don't feel like it, because that is when you need it most.'

You probably remember playing with iron filings at school. You run a magnet over a bunch of iron filings and they all stand to attention, or move to the right or to the left. Long before the magnet makes physical contact with the filings, something is happening. Why? Because an invisible power, magnetism, is affecting them.

In the same way, prayer, which is invisible and spiritual, affects that which is visible and physical.

Prayer and action

A priest in a poor inner city area desperately needed money for a new church building. At his wits' end, he pleaded with God: 'Lord, if you love me, let me win the national lottery this week!' Saturday was the grand draw, but there was nothing for the priest.

He went back to church to plead with God again: 'Lord, if you love me, let me win the national lottery this week!' But at the end of the week, another winner was announced.

A third time he returned to pray at the altar: 'Lord, if you love me, let me win the national lottery this week!' As he got up to go, a voice boomed from the heavens: 'OK. But meet me half-way. This week, buy a lottery ticket!'

'I sometimes think he tries a bit too hard
at family services!!'

Prayers answered

I asked God for strength, that I might achieve.
I was made weak, that I might learn humbly to
  obey.

I asked for health, that I might do greater things.
I was given infirmity, that I might do better
  things.

I asked for riches, that I might be happy.
I was given poverty, that I might be wise.

I asked for power, that I might have the praise
  of men.
I was given weakness, that I might feel the need
  of God.

I asked for all things that I might enjoy life,
I was given life that I might enjoy all things.

I got nothing that I asked for — but everything
  that I had hoped for.
Almost, despite myself, my unspoken prayers
  were answered.
I am, among all men, most richly blessed.

Anonymous Confederate soldier
of the American Civil War

Preachers and preaching

A rather timid minister was told by one part of
the congregation to preach 'the old-fashioned
gospel', and by the rest to be more broadminded.
One day he got up to preach and ended up
saying, 'Unless you repent, in a measure, and are
saved, so to speak, you are, I am sorry to say, in
danger of hell-fire and damnation, to a certain
extent.'

Now I lay me down to sleep;
The sermon's long and the subject deep;
If he gets through before I wake,
Someone give me a gentle shake.

On accepting his first church, a young pastor
asked an elderly board member if he had any
wise advice. The elderly man responded, 'Son, a
sermon is like a good meal; you should end it
just before we have had enough.'

My preacher's eyes I've never seen
Though the light in them may shine,
For when he prays, he closes his,
And when he preaches, I close mine.

The vicar was hoping to get a discount on the price of a suit.

'I'm just a poor preacher!' he said to the shop keeper.

'Yes, I know,' the shop keeper replied. 'I've heard you preach.'

Little girl to mummy: 'Mummy, why does the pastor pray before his sermon?'

She replied, 'He's asking God to help him preach a good sermon.'

'Mummy, why doesn't God answer his prayer?'

During a long and very boring sermon, a small but distinct voice could be heard at the back of the church, asking:

'Mummy, is it still Sunday?'

George Whitefield, the great eighteenth-century preacher, told a story about the most famous actor of his day, David Garrick.

A preacher asked him, 'How is it that you actors are able, on the stage, to produce so great an effect with fiction; whilst we preachers, in the pulpit, obtain such a small result with the facts?'

Garrick replied, 'I suppose it is because we present fiction as though it were fact, whilst you, too often, offer facts as though they were fiction.'

A visiting preacher was aware that he had overstepped the mark with his 45-minute sermon.

'I'm so sorry', he explained to the verger, 'but there wasn't a clock in front of me', to which the verger replied, 'No, but there was a calendar behind you.'

Church member to minister:
'You'll never know what your sermon meant to me. It was like water to a drowning man!'

Preacher: Can everyone hear me at the back?
Voice from the back:
Yes, but I wouldn't mind changing seats with someone who can't.

Orators are most vehement when their cause is weak.

                                        Cicero

For goodness' sake, George! You're on holiday!

On the frequent lack of application to life of the text: We often speak eloquently of the general state of the rubber industry in the West, when people simply want to know how to mend a flat tyre!

Preaching/Reconciliation

Bishop Festo Kivengere told the story of how he was going off to preach after a row with his wife. The Holy Spirit said to him, 'Go back and pray with your wife!'

He argued, 'I'm due to preach in twenty minutes. I'll do it afterwards.'

'OK,' said the Holy Spirit. 'You go and preach; I'll stay with your wife.'

Preaching (bad preaching)

'My lips are hermeneutically sealed.'

Well, the minister got to know a *little* Greek and Hebrew while he was at College. The Greek ran the kebab shop and the Hebrew made his suits!

"If God had meant Christians to think,
he'd have given them brains."

His preaching cost nothing — and it was worth it!

Mark Twain

Predestination

Then there was the Calvinist who fell down the stairs and said, 'thank goodness that's over with!'

Prepared?

The 'kairos' moment

An unemployed actor finally landed a one-line part in a big West End play. He only had five words to say; 'Hark! How the cannons roar!' and spent all his time practicing different ways of saying it.

On the morning of the first day of the performance he ate his breakfast, muttering, 'Hark! How the cannons roar!' As he caught the tube into the city he repeated to himself, 'Hark! How the cannons roar!' Finally, as he stood in the wings waiting for his moment to come, he said over and over, 'Hark! How the cannons roar!'

At last the moment came. He walked on stage and his cue came, 'Bang!'

'What was that!?' he cried.

Principles

When a man approves of something in principle it means he hasn't the slightest intention of putting it into practice.

Bismarck

Procrastination

The Devil doesn't care how much good we do, as long as we don't do it today.

> Procrastination is my sin,
> It brings me naught but sorrow.
> I know that I should stop it,
> In fact, I will — tomorrow!
>
> *Gloria Pitzer*

Why put off till tomorrow what you can safely put off till the week after next?

A woman leaves a pair of shoes she rarely uses at the mender's and only remembers two years later when she finds the ticket in her purse. She takes it in to the shop, rather apologetically.

'Ah yes, Mrs Smith' says the cobbler. They'll be ready next Monday.'

Prophecy

H L Mencken, an American journalist covering a rather dull and, he thought, predictable Presidential convention meeting, sent the Press Release the day before. However, a crucial issue in the meeting went quite the other way from what was expected. Mencken cabled the newspaper office with the simple instruction: 'Insert "not" as sense requires.'

Prophecy (false)

'Thus says the Lord: I have nothing against you . . . as far as I know . . .'

Purpose

God has created me
to do him some definite serivce.
He has committed some work to me
which he has not
committed to another.
I have my mission.
I may never know it in this life,
but I shall be told it in the next.
I am a link in a chain,
a bond of connection between persons.
He has not created me for naught;
I shall do good — I shall do his work;
I shall be an angel of peace,
a preacher of truth in my own place
while not intending it
if I do but keep his commandments.
Therefore I will trust him.
Whatever I am, I can never be thrown away.
If I am in sickness, my sickness may serve him;
in perplexity, my perplexity may serve him,
if I am in sorrow, my sorrow may serve him.
He does nothing in vain.
He knows what he is about.
He may take away my friends,
he may throw me among strangers,
he may make me feel desolate,
make my spirits sink,
hide my future from me — still
He knows what he is about.

Cardinal Newman

R

Rebellion

A father repeatedly told his little boy to sit down on the back seat of the car. He remained standing until eventually, exasperated, the father physically sat the boy down.

The little boy grimaced, and muttered, 'I may be sitting down on the outside, but I'm standing up on the inside!'

Relationships

Bakker started out loving people and using things, but then he started loving things and using people.

Jerry Miller, Prosecutor at fraud trial of Jim Bakker

Repentance

A painter not particularly noted for his honesty decided to water down the paint but charge his customer for the full amount he should have used. Unfortunately for him, he carried the process rather too far with the result that the finished work looked so bad that even the most short-sighted client would notice it.

'What can I do now?' he wailed.

From the heavens a great voice boomed, 'Repaint! And thin no more!'

A new Christian wrote to the Inland Revenue: 'I can't sleep at night, so I am enclosing £100 I forgot to declare.

PS. If I still can't sleep, I will send the rest.'

It was bank holiday weekend and a long queue had formed at the petrol station. When at last it was the vicar's turn, the attendant apologised for the long delay: 'They knew they were going to make this trip, yet they all waited until the last minute to get ready!'

The vicar smiled ruefully. 'I know what you mean', he said. 'It's like that in my business, too!'

Doctor to overweight patient: 'Here's a list of what you must eat: lettuce, carrots, cabbage . . .'

'That's fine, doctor', interrupted the patient, 'but do I take them before or after meals?'

A deacon, frequently called on to pray at the church prayer meeting, always concluded his prayer, 'And now, Lord, clean all the cobwebs out of our lives.'

The others knew what he meant — all the little unsightly words, thoughts and deeds that we let accumulate in our lives. Finally it got too much for one of the brethren who had heard that prayer many times. So on hearing it again, he jumped to his feet and shouted, 'Don't do it, Lord! Kill the spider!'

Research

If you steal from another, it's plagiarism. If you steal from many, it's research.

Responsibility

Young boy to his father, who is reading his appalling end-of-term report: 'What do you think the trouble is, Dad? Heredity or environment?

Risk-taking

God equipped us with necks — we should
occasionally stick them out!

If you don't go overboard, you tend not to make
a splash.

S

Salvation

The Pit

A man fell into a pit and couldn't get himself out.

A *subjective* person came along and said, 'I feel for you down there.'

An *objective* person came along and said, 'It's logical that someone would fall down there.'

A *Pharisee* said, 'Only bad people fall into pits.'

A *news reporter* wanted the exclusive story on the man's pit.

Confucius said, 'If you had listened to me, you wouldn't be in that pit.'

Buddha said, 'Your pit is only a state of mind.'

A *realist* said, 'That's a PIT.'

A *scientist* calculated the pressure necessary (PSI) to get him out of the pit.

A *geologist* told him to appreciate the rock strata in the pit.

A *tax man* asked if he was paying taxes on the pit.

The council inspector asked if he had a permit to dig a pit.

An *evasive* person came along and avoided the subject of his pit altogether.

A *self-pitying* person said, 'You haven't seen anything until you've seem MY pit!'

A *charismatic* said, 'Just confess that you're not in a pit.'

An *optimist* said, 'Things could be worse.'

A *pessimist* said, 'Things will get worse.'

Jesus, seeing the man, took him by the hand and lifted him out of the pit.

Kenneth D Filkins

Salvation is moving from living death to deathless life.

Jack Odell

Second Coming of Christ

I've no idea when Jesus is coming back. I'm on the Welcoming Committee, not the Planning Committee.

Tony Campolo

Secularisation

The first Law of Secularisation: 'Hollywood loves you and has a marvellous plan for your life.'

Self-pity

Self-pity is our worst enemy and, if we yield to it,
we can never do anything wise in the world.

Hellen Keller

Selfishness

The two men were desperately running for their
lives, pursued by a great grizzly bear. Suddenly
one stopped to put on some running shoes.

'You'll never outrun the bear!' explained the
other man in bewilderment.

'I don't have to outrun the bear,' explained his
friend, 'I only have to outrun you.'

Self sacrifice

The trouble with a living sacrifice is that it keeps
crawling off the altar!

He is no fool who gives up what he cannot keep
to gain what he can never lose.

Jim Elliot

Sermons

One Sunday morning, the vicar apologised to his congregation for the sticking-plaster on his face. 'I was thinking about my sermon and cut my face,' he said.

Afterwards, in the collection plate he found a note that read, 'Next time, why not think about your face and cut the sermon?'

A vicar about to speak at a formal dinner was announced by the MC with the words, 'Pray for the silence of the Reverend Smith.'

Several years ago the *British Weekly* printed a letter to the editor:

'Dear Sir,
I notice that ministers seem to set a great deal of importance on their sermons and spend a great deal of time in preparing them. I have been attending services quite regularly for the past thirty years and during that time, if I estimate correctly, I have listened to no less than three thousand sermons. But, to my consternation, I discover I cannot remember a single one of them. I wonder if a minister's

*Good morning — I have a sermon-a-gram
for you!!*

time might be more profitably spent on
something else?
    Yours sincerely . . .'

That letter triggered an avalanche of angry
responses for weeks. Sermons were castigated
and defended by lay people and clergy, but
eventually a single letter closed the debate:

'Dear Sir,
I have been married for thirty years. During
that time I have eaten 32,000 meals — mostly
of my wife's cooking. Suddenly, I have
discovered that I cannot remember the menu
of a single meal. And yet, I received
nourishment from every one of them. I have
the distinct impression that without them I
would have starved to death long ago.
    Yours sincerely . . .'

James Berkley

A little boy in church asked his father, as the
offering bags came round, 'Daddy, what does
that mean?'
    'They're collecting our money for God.'
    As they knelt for prayer, the little boy asked,
'Daddy, what does that mean?'
    'It means we're talking to God.'
    And when the minister removed his watch at
the start of the sermon, laying it in front of him

on the pulpit, the little boy asked, 'Daddy, what does that mean?'

'Absolutely nothing!'

After a rather long and dull sermon the preacher asked a deacon, 'Do you think I should have put more fire in my sermon?'

'You should have put more sermon in the fire!' he replied.

'I don't mind people looking at their watches while I'm preaching, but I get worried when they take them off and shake them!'

A sermon doesn't have to be eternal to be immortal.

'I don't mind people looking at their watches when I preach, but it worries me when they get out their diaries.'

A good sermon leaves you wondering how the preacher knew so much about you.

Service

All the holy men seem to have gone off and died. There's no one left but us sinners to carry on the ministry.

Jamie Buckingham

I take comfort from the fact that it was willing amateurs who built the Ark, whereas professionals built the *Titanic*.

I don't know what your destiny will be but one thing I know, the only ones among you who will be really happy are those who have sought and found how to serve.

Albert Schweitzer

Seven deadly sins

E Stanley Jones, an American missionary, statesman, author and lecturer, formulated what he called the seven deadly sins:

> Politics without principle,
> Wealth without work,
> Pleasure without conscience,
> Knowledge without character,
> Business without morality,
> Science without humanity,
> Worship without sacrifice.

Shared leadership

As a busy mother commented, 'It took me a lot longer to make breakfast this morning. My children helped me!'

Sin

On the church notice board was a poster which read: 'Are you tired of sin? Then come inside.'

Underneath someone had added, 'If not, phone Bayswater 23769.'

Sin: putting worst things first.

Joseph Gancher

I'm more afraid of my own heart than of the Pope and all his cardinals!

Martin Luther

You cannot play with sin and overcome it at the same time.

J C Macaulay

Sin's consequences

Most of us spend the first six days of each week sowing wild oats and the seventh praying for a crop failure.

Sincerity

It was the great Methodist evangelist, John Wesley, who told his young preachers: 'Don't worry about how to get crowds. Just get on fire and the people will come to see you burn.'

I see covetousness has risen to number three!

He had all the sincerity of a Colonel Sanders
looking the chicken in the eye and saying, 'Trust
me!'

Single-mindedness

> Do all the good you can
> By all the means you can
> In all the ways you can
> In all the places you can
> At all the times you can
> To all the people you can
> As long as ever you can.
>
> *John Wesley*

Sorrow

Lessons from Sorrow

I walked a mile with Pleasure;
She chatted all the way,
But left me none the wiser
For all she had to say.

I walked a mile with Sorrow
And ne'er a word said she;
But, oh, the things I learned from her
When Sorrow walked with me.

Earth has no sorrow that heaven cannot heal.

Thomas Moore

How else but through a broken heart
May Lord Christ enter in?

Oscar Wilde
in 'The Ballad of Reading Gaol'

Sovereignty of God

At a minister's induction, the order of service declared that the hymn before the 'Act of Induction' would be, 'Our God resigns'.

Standing up for the faith

A police sergeant with a class of cadets asked, 'Imagine you're on duty when two cars smash into each other. You are just about to go to their aid when you notice an articulated lorry heading down the hill towards this blind corner where the accident occurred. You hear a scream and see that the shock of the crash has sent a pregnant woman on the pavement into premature labour. Meanwhile, a fireball from one of the car's petrol tanks is heading towards a crowded pub full of under-age drinkers. What do you do?'

An intelligent young cadet spoke up, 'Slip off my uniform and merge with the crowd, sarge!'

A great oak is only a little nut that held its ground.

Stand-ins

As the substitute preacher stood in the pulpit he noticed a piece of old cardboard filling in the gap in a beautiful, but broken, stained-glass window.

'You know,' he said, 'standing in for such an eminent preacher today, I feel a bit like that cardboard in the stained-glass window — a poor substitute for the real thing.'

After the service, one of the congregation greeted him warmly at the door: 'I want you to know,' he said, 'that you weren't a piece of cardboard this morning — you were a real pane!'

The curate had stepped in to take the sermon at very short notice, because the vicar was ill. At the end of the sermon he explained apologetically, 'At such short notice I'm afraid I

just had to rely on the Holy Spirit. Next week I
hope to do better!'

Stress

When the going gets tough,
the tough go shopping.

Leaders should always remember that,
'God loves you and everyone else
has a marvellous plan for your life!'

She was the kind of woman who made the Statue
of Liberty look like someone you could relax
with.

Success

If at first you don't succeed . . . so much for sky-
diving.

The worst that can happen to a man is to succeed before he is ready.

Martin Lloyd-Jones

Only in a dictionary does success come before work.

Success is never final, failure never fatal. It's courage that counts.

When I try, I fail. When I trust, He succeeds.

Stewardship

The huge, brass offertory plates were passed around the congregation one Sunday evening — and returned almost empty to the vicar. He took them, held them up to heaven and prayed, 'Lord, we thank you for the safe return of these plates . . .'

Suffering

Job needed a doctor, but they sent him social workers!

The Weaver

My life is but a weaving between my Lord and
   me,
I cannot choose the colours he worketh steadily.
Oft times he weaveth sorrow, and I in foolish
   pride
Forget he sees the upper and I the underside.

Not till the loom is silent and the shuttle ceased
   to fly,
Shall God unroll the canvas and explain the
   reason why
The dark threads are as needful in the weaver's
   skilful hand,
As the threads of gold and silver, in the pattern
   he has planned.

When you struggle in the darkness, don't forget
what you heard in the light.

Sunday trading

'The merchants and tradesmen camped outside Jerusalem once or twice, but I spoke sharply to them and said, "What are you doing out here, camping round the wall? If you do this again, I will arrest you." And that was the last time they came on the Sabbath.'

Nehemiah 13:2–21, Living Bible

Tact

Tact is the art of making a point without making an enemy.

Howard W Newton

Teamwork

Fred's never been much of a sportsman. When he played in goal at football the team called him Cinderella because he kept missing the ball.

Temptation

It is startling to think that Satan can actually come into the heart of a man in such close touch with Jesus as Judas was. And more — he is cunningly trying to do it today. Yet he can only get in through a door opened from the inside. Every man controls the door of his own life. Satan can't get in without our help.

S D Gordon

When you flee temptation, be sure you don't leave a forwarding address!

Thinking

As long as the devil can keep us terrified of thinking, he will always limit the work of God in our souls.

Oswald Chambers

If God had meant Christians to think, he'd have given them brains.

Reading moulds thinking. As I scan my shelves I spot those books other than the Bible that have influenced my personal thought and ministry, particularly my battle not to become secularized. Unless we maintain constant companionship with Christians who direct our thinking Christianly, we easily fall prey to the spirit of the times.

Katie Wiebe

A great many people think they are thinking when they are merely rearranging their prejudices.

William James

Thoroughness

He went through it like a twelve-year-old inspecting his moustache.

Tradition

Tradition is the living faith of the dead. Honour it! Traditionalism is the dead faith of the living. Abandon it!

Transformation

The audience was waiting for the brilliant pianist
to come out onto the stage. Then, to everyone's
embarrassment, a little boy wandered up onto
the stage and started banging out one, harsh note
on the *Steinway*. Suddenly, the maestro appeared
in the wings and made his way over to the boy.

Standing behind him as he banged away
tunelessly, he began to weave a melody around
the note, taking it up into his larger tune and
transforming it into something beautiful. After a
few moments, the maestro gently led the boy
away from the piano and together they took a
bow to the audience's applause. The little boy
wandered back to his seat — not embarassed,
not having been made to look foolish.

In the same way, Jesus can take the harsh,
discordant, out-of-tune moments of our lives —
perhaps a time of sexual sin, or of cowardice or
defeat in some other way — and can weave his
own purposes around them. As we let him do
this, he transforms our mistakes and failures,
bringing out of them something he can use for
his glory.

Translations

On the dangers inherent in translating: One
Russian interpreter didn't quite know what to

make of, 'The spirit is willing but the flesh is weak,' and translated it by, 'the vodka is good but the meat is bad!'

Trust

Never trust a man who, when left alone in a room with a tea cosy, doesn't try it on.

A man fell off a cliff but managed to grab hold of a branch on his way down. He hung there and shouted up to the top, 'Is anybody up there?'
   'Yes,' came the reply, 'God is up here!'
   'Can you help me, God?'
   'Yes.'
   'What do you want me to do?'
   'Let go of the branch.'
   There was a pause.
   'Is there anybody else up there?'

There's only one thing better than a friend you can trust, and that's a friend who trusts you.

'Er . . . this is so embarrassing — it's stuck!'

Even if you think you have someone eating out of your hand, it's still advisable to count your fingers afterwards!

Truth

A lie can travel halfway around the world while the truth is putting on its shoes.

Mark Twain

Men occasionally stumble over the truth, but most of them pick themselves up and hurry off as if nothing had happened.

Winston Churchill

$\mathcal{V}$

Values — relative and absolute

Norman was the man at the factory who sounded the hooter to say when work began and finished. Every morning as he walked past the jewellers, he set his watch by the big clock in the window. One day his watch went wrong so, on the way home from work, he took it into the jewellers for mending. Next morning he picked it up and, as he was leaving the shop, put his watch right by the big clock in the window.

'Yes, I know that's always right,' said the watchmaker. 'I set it every morning by the factory hooter.'

Verbosity

In a small trumpet blast against bureaucratic verbosity, this list is circulating around Government departments in Washington:

The Lord's Prayer: 56 words.
The twenty-third Psalm: 118 words.
The Gettysburg address: 226 words.
The ten commandments: 297 words.

The United States Department of Agriculture
  Order on the price of cabbage: 15,629 words.

Vision

We think too small, like the frog at the bottom of
the well. He thinks the sky is only as big as the
top of the well. If he surfaced, he would have an
entirely different view.

Mao Tse-Tung

Our task now is not to fix the blame for the past,
but to fix the course for the future.

John F Kennedy

The man who misses all the fun
Is he who says, 'It can't be done.'
In solemn pride, he stands aloof
And greets each venture with reproof.
Had he the power, he would efface
The history of the human race.
We'd have no radio, no cars,
No streets lit by electric stars;
No telegraph, no telephone;
We'd linger in the age of stone.
The world would sleep if things were run
By folks who say, 'It can't be done.'

It is for us to pray not for tasks equal to our powers, but for powers equal to our tasks; to go forward with a great desire forever beating at the door of our hearts as we travel toward our distant goal.

Helen Keller

Will

The secret of an unsettled life lies too often in an unsurrendered will.

Will of God

When David Livingstone was asked if he was afraid that going into Africa would be too difficult and too dangerous, he answered, 'I am immortal until the will of God for me is accomplished.'

Wisdom

There had never been any argument about it:
Fred was the wisest and shrewdest man in town.
One day a young lad in the community
questioned him about it.

'Fred, what is it that makes you so wise?' he
asked.

'Good judgment,' replied Fred, readily. 'I'd say
it was my good judgment.'

'And where did you get your good judgment?'

'That I got from experience.'

'Where did you get your experience?'

'From my bad judgment.'

Wise living

A pilot came aboard a large tanker to help bring
it into harbour. The captain asked him if he really
knew where all the rocks were. 'No,' he replied,
'but I know where there aren't any!'

Witness

The sixteenth-century bishop, Hugh Latimer,
was one of the first preachers of social
righteousness in the English-speaking world. He

was imprisoned for his denunciations of social and ecclesiastical abuses. While in the Tower of London he wrote, 'Pray for me; I say, pray for me. At times I am so afraid that I could creep into a mousehole.' This was the same Latimer who later walked bravely to the stake in Oxford, saying to his companion, Nicholas Ridley, as he went, 'Play the man, Master Ridley; we shall this day light such a candle, by God's grace, in England, as I trust shall never be put out.'

Women

The Baptist church deacons decided to invite their woman minister to go fishing with them. They were fifty yards or so from the shore when she said, apologetically, 'I'm sorry — I've forgotten my fishing rod!'

So she hopped out of the boat, walked across the water to the bank and picked up the rod. As she strolled back one deacon was heard to mutter, 'Typical of a woman — always forgetting things!'

Words

> I try to watch the words I say,
> And keep them soft and sweet;
> For I don't know from day to day,
> Which ones I'll have to eat!

Work

The Pope was asked on one occasion, 'How many people work here at the Vatican?' He replied, 'Oh, about half of them.'

Worldliness

The Christian is not ruined by living in the world but by the world living in him.

Worry

Ulcers are caused not by what you eat, but by what's eating you!

You can't change the past but you can spoil the present by worrying about the future.

When I look back on all these worries, I remember the story of the old man who said, on his deathbed, that he had a lot of trouble in his life, most of which never happened.

Sir Winston Churchill

Young people

Some things never change . . .

The children now love luxury; they show disrespect for elders and love chatter in the place of exercise. Children are tyrants, not the servants of their households. They no longer rise when their elders enter the room. They contradict their parents, chatter before company, gobble up dainties at the table, cross their legs and tyrannise their teachers.

Socrates, 469–399 BC

I see no hope for the future of our people if they are dependent on the frivolous youth of today, for certainly all youth are reckless beyond words . . . When I was young we were taught to be discreet and respectful of elders, but the present youth are exceedingly impatient of restraint.

Hesiod, Greek poet, eighth-century BC